j973   MORRIS, RICHARD BRANDON
        THE INDIAN WARS.
        (REV. ED. c1985)

D0572568

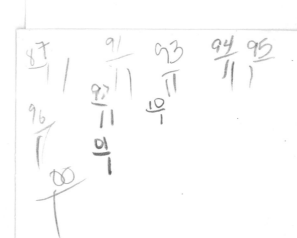

AMERICAN HISTORY TOPIC BOOKS

THE INDIAN WARS

Richard B. Morris

Illustrations by Leonard Everett Fisher

Lerner Publications Company   Minneapolis

For Caroline,
a granddaughter of the West,
where the memories of our First Americans are poignant
reminders of this nation's commitment to justice for all

1985 REVISED EDITION

Revised edition copyright © 1985 by Lerner Publications Company.
Published by arrangement with Lou Reda Productions, Inc.
First published as *The First Book of the Indian Wars.*

Library of Congress Cataloging in Publication Data

Morris, Richard Brandon, 1904-
      The Indian wars.

      (American history topic books)
      Rev. ed. of: The first book of the Indian wars.
c1959.
      Includes index.
      Summary: Describes Indian warfare in colonial
times, with an emphasis on Indian activity in the wars
among the white colonists.
      1. Indians of North America — Wars — Juvenile
literature. [1. Indians of North America — Wars]
I. Fisher, Leonard Everett, ill.   II. Morris, Richard
Brandon, 1904-   .   First book of the Indian wars.
III.   Title.   IV. Series.
E82.M67   1985   973   85-12994
ISBN 0-8225-1703-5 (lib. bdg.)

Manufactured in the United States of America

    2 3 4 5 6 7 8 9 10 94 93 92 91 90 89 88 87 00

CONTENTS

INDIAN TRIBES
OF THE UNITED STATES
WHEN THE WHITE MAN ARRIVED

EXPLORERS AND COLONIZERS

French . . . . . . English _ _ _
Spanish _ . _ . _ Dutch + + +

NORTHWEST COAST

Chohali
Chinook
Klikitat
Spokane
Flathead
Nez Percé
Bannock
Yakima
Coos
Klamath
Modoc
Snake
Arapho
Shasta
Cheyenne
Shoshone

GREAT

BASIN

Paiute
Ute
Kiowa

Miwok

Salinan

CALIFORNIA

CLIFF DWELLERS

Navajo

Hopi

Pueblo

Mojave

SOUTHWEST

Yuma

Apache

Pima

Comanche

Apache

Coahiltecos

PACIFIC

OCEAN

1578

Blackfoot

Arapho

Crow

Dakota

Ponca

GREAT PLAINS

FAR

Pawnee

N
W E
S

INTRODUCTION TO REVISED EDITION

The first Americans who settled the North American continent are known as the Indians. They consisted of many different peoples and were organized into many different tribes. They did not look alike, and they spoke a variety of languages. Some lived at peace with their neighbors, while others were more warlike. They had their own beliefs and ways of life that were well suited to the forests, to the prairies, or to the plains where they lived.

The coming of the Europeans proved a great shock to the Indians. They were not prepared for the white settlers' way of life. They were angered by the settlers' land grabbing, by their fenced-in farms, and, most of all, by their ever-increasing numbers.

These differences created friction between the Indians and the whites. When it came to bargaining, the Indians were no match for the Europeans. The European settlers made and broke many treaties with the Indians, who were pushed westward from settlement to settlement. When the Indians stood and fought bravely, they were finally defeated. Eventually, the way of life of the American Indian was very largely destroyed.

Today, we have a better understanding of the problems the Indians faced as the white settlers spread across North America. We admire the Indians' effort to keep some of the continent for themselves and to preserve lands sacred to them by tradition. The nation and the states are attempting to make up for the losses the American Indian has suffered from broken treaties and bad faith. Surely, America without the Indians would be a much poorer country.

WARRIOR AND MAN OF PEACE

Ever since the West was settled, children have played "cowboys and Indians." When they have thought of the Indian, they have thought of a warrior and fighter and of a special kind of fighter—one who is always shouting the warcry against peaceful white settlers and who attacks from ambush, makes war on helpless people, and takes the scalps of old and young alike.

Now, this is by no means a fair picture of the Indian. They passed the pipe of peace at their councils as often as they raised the tomahawk. They were explorers, discoverers, hunters, trappers, and farmers. They were the first to discover America, the first to learn the secrets of this vast continent. They were the first to cut the trees and plow the land. From the Indian, the white settlers learned about the streams and trails of America. They learned how to plant Indian corn, squash, pumpkins, peanuts, and other important foods we raise today. From the Indian, the settlers learned how to dress for the woods and how to travel on the inland waters. The hunting shirt, the moccasin, and the canoe were all taken over from the Indian by the white settlers.

But this book will tell about the Indian as a warrior. Many Indians regarded fighting as a game and enjoyed war. Others went on the warpath for very much the same reasons that the white settlers went to war. They fought to defend themselves and their dear ones. They fought for power over other tribes. They were driven to war by hunger. All these reasons for war existed before the coming of the white settlers.

The colonists' coming made a big difference in the life of the Indians. They now adopted many of the white settlers' ways of hunting, farming, and even cooking. They now needed the guns made by the settlers instead of the bows and arrows they had made for themselves. In fact, some Indians forgot entirely how to hunt with bow and arrow. The Indian found the settlers' knives, hoes, and axes far superior to their own stone implements, and the iron and copper kettles the settlers brought along much more practicable for cooking than the pottery jars they had ben using. They found it a lot easier to buy ready-made blankets than to weave them for themselves. And, for the first time, Indians were exposed to alcohol and the European diseases brought to America by the colonists.

The Indians sold the white settlers the furs they trapped in exchange for European goods. They also sold the settlers something else they wanted very badly— land. When the people from rival European nations went to war with each other over this very land, they looked to the Indians for help. The Indians generally took the side of those who offered them the best trade goods at the best price and who seemed least likely to threaten the lands they still held. The part the Indians played in these wars helped decide who was to win the continent of America.

THE INDIAN DISCOVERS AMERICA

At least twenty thousand years ago, the Indians began coming to America. They crossed over from Siberia into Alaska. They were Stone Age people. The first ones who came over did not even have bows and arrows. They hunted with spears and javelins. They kept crossing from Asia over a long period of time. They did not even look alike, and they spoke different languages. Some were darker than others, but most of them had a yellowish ivory skin. When the skin tanned, it turned a strong brown. The first white people along the Atlantic coast found Indians whose skin burned to a copper color. They called them "red men," but, in fact, white people's skin is usually redder, especially when sunburned.

The Indians settled both North and South America. In what are now Mexico and Peru, they built great civilizations. They had wonderful cities, magnificent temples, a knowledge of mathematics and astronomy, and even a form of writing.

The Indians who settled in what is now the United

Some of them became village or pueblo dwellers.

4

States were much less advanced than those in Mexico and Peru. But bit by bit, they learned things from their neighbors farther south. Among other things, they learned how to farm and how to build, and, with this knowledge, some of them became village or *pueblo* dwellers. *Pueblo* is the Spanish word for village.

Many of the Pueblo tribes of the Southwest lived in villages of stone houses cemented with a local clay called *adobe*. Others lived on the ledges of cliffs where fiercer tribes could not attack them easily. We call these Indians the Cliff Dwellers.

In the Southeast from the coast of the Gulf of Mexico up the Mississippi River almost to the Great Lakes, were the Mound Builders. These Indians got their name from the great mounds of rubble they built. This rubble was covered with earth, and the finished mounds look somewhat like the pyramids of Central America. Among the most famous of the Mound Builders was the Natchez tribe. The Natchez were ruled by a king called "The Sun."

THE ALGONQUINS

In this book, we are chiefly concerned with the three great groups of Indians along the Atlantic coast—the Algonquins, the Iroquois, and the so-called Five Civilized

Tribes. The Algonquins were hunters and fishermen and lived in small, scattered villages. For shelter, they built wigwams by bending poles to form dome-shaped frames. Over the frames, they placed birchbark or woven mats. They also built tepees where the poles were arranged to form a cone. Over the cone, bark was laid.

The Algonquins were divided into two groups. One group lived along the coast from Canada to Virginia and from the Atlantic to the Appalachian Mountains. The other dwelt west of the mountains in the region of the Great Lakes and in lower Canada.

THE IROQUOIS

It was the fierce and warlike Iroquois who divided the Algonquins. These invaders had probably come up from the south and west and driven a wedge into Algonquin territory. Unlike the Algonquins, the Iroquois were bound together by close ties. They were actually a league of five tribes ("The Five Nations")—the Senecas, the Cayugas, the Onondagas, the Oneidas, and the Mohawks. These tribes had banded together around the year 1570 to end warfare. They called their league "The Great Peace." A great Indian leader named Deganawida is supposed to have thought of the league first, but laws and organiza-

While the white men thought of battles in terms of large armies arrayed against each other, the Indians struck before great numbers had been assembled. Their usual method of attack was the raid, and they usually picked on ome lonely village or group of cabins.

Before a raid took place, the war chief would summon e war party to an assembly, or powwow, after which the ves danced and prayed. Then they would make their stealthily through the woods to let loose their attack efore dawn. Horrible shrieks from the raiders sig- the attack. They might set the enemy's houses afire rning arrows, or push burning wagons up against led fort. Then they would rush in and kill the de- s they ran out of their homes in panic.

distance, the Indians had always used long bows ng arrows. At close quarters, they used spears, ahawks. But when the white man came, the ally shifted from bows and arrows to firearms. of the seventeenth century, the French, the English were all trading guns and ammu- the North, the Indians made the change rows to muskets faster than in the South. e Indian warriors in New England relied uns. In the South, guns did not replace with all tribes until about 1730. But ys an advantage to the Indian. An

tion were worked out by his follower, the Indian hero Hiawatha. The league lasted for three hundred years. Acting together, the Iroquois were a powerful confederacy.

The French, when they came to Canada, backed the Algonquins and the Hurons, who lived in what is now the province of Ontario. The Dutch, and after them the English, made allies of the Iroquois and armed them to fight the French and their Indian friends. Had it not been for these two alliances, the whole history of North America might well have been different.

The poles were arranged to form a cone.

THE FIVE CIVILIZED TRIBES

In the Southeast, the most famous and warlike Indians were the Creeks, Chickasaws, Choctaws, Cherokees, and Seminoles. They have been called the "Five Civilized Tribes" because much later on in the early nineteenth century, they made great progress in learning how to read and write. This was largely due to the efforts of a Cherokee genius named Sequoyah.

The Five Civilized Tribes were not as closely united as the Iroquois. The Creeks, for example, were really a confederacy of tribes who spoke the same language, and they would often fight together against other tribes. But these alliances did not last.

The three great European powers, Spain, France, and England, all pushed into territory held by the Five Civilized Tribes. The Spaniards took over Florida. The French settled along the lower Mississippi and in New Orleans. The British settled on the frontier of South Carolina and Georgia.

In dealing with the European nations, the Five Civilized Tribes did not put up a united front. The Creeks entered into alliance with the English. The Choctaws threw in their lot with the French. Since England was the winner in her wars against France and Spain, the Creeks made a lucky choice of an ally and became the strongest Indian

power in the Southeast. When the American P broke out the Creeks fought with the Eng' the Patriots.

HOW THE INDIANS FOUGHT

From childhood, the young I for fighting. He would have to hood. He would be forced to the woods with only bow knife to defend himself a had to take other tests order to prove he w or Indian fighter. W ready to join the Creeks, every If he failed, a wife.

The In men. T fough roc t v But and again.

The braves danced and prayed.

Indian warrior could shoot several arrows a minute in silence. In the same time, he could get off not more than one round of shot, and he made a great noise in doing so. Not only that, but the more Indians counted on guns and powder, the more dependent they were on the European powers to supply them.

Western movies usually show Indians riding fast horses to attack slow-moving covered wagon trains. That was true of the nineteenth century but bear in mind that horses were not known to the American Indian until the Europeans brought them to America. The Indians began to use them in the seventeenth century, but seldom used them in fighting in colonial times.

Warfare between Indians and whites was indeed terrifying. To prove their success in a raid, Indians would take their victims' scalps. Colonists would do the same with Indian victims, and they could even get money from their colony for every scalp they brought back.

Women and children were often not spared by Indians or by white people. At times, Indians took them prisoner and adopted them into their tribes. But when they took a warrior prisoner, it was chiefly to torture him. They would tie him to a pole in the middle of their village and torture him to death, usually by roasting him slowly over a fire. These Indian prisoners died bravely. Often they would sing war songs and taunt their captors.

When they took a warrior prisoner it was chiefly to torture him.

At the start of the wars between whites and Indians, white captives, too, were tortured to death. Later, the Indians found it more profitable to hold white captives for ransom. The white settlers took up collections to redeem their friends and relatives.

White men had to find out the hard way that in fighting Indians one had to use Indian ways. Carry few rations and live off the land as the Indians did. Use scouts when going through the woods. Avoid ambush. Attack by surprise. Set fire to Indian forts and destroy Indian corn fields and food supplies. Learn how to shoot kneeling and lying down, to swim, to use snowshoes.

In the long run, the white man had advantages over the Indian. He used the bayonet in close attack and fired cannon in sieges. Neither weapon was used by the Indians. Better organization, greater numbers, and better weapons spelled victory in the end for the white man.

Three of the greatest Patriot fighters in the American Revolution learned a great deal from fighting against the Indians before the Revolution started. They were George Washington, who had fought the Indians at the Forks of the Ohio during the French and Indian War, Francis Marion, known as the "Swamp Fox," who had battled the Cherokees on the Southern frontier, and George Rogers Clark, conqueror of the old Northwest, who had fought Indians in Kentucky during Lord Dunmore's War.

14

THE COMING OF THE WHITE MAN

Once the news of Columbus's voyages spread in Europe, white colonists did not take long to settle in North America. The Spaniards set foot on North America first—in Florida in 1513, then in the Southwest, and lastly along the California coast. The French moved up the St. Lawrence Valley to begin their settlement of Canada. Toward the end of the sixteenth century, the English began to make serious plans to settle along the Atlantic coast. They finally succeeded in getting a foothold at Jamestown in 1607. The Dutch followed shortly upon Henry Hudson's voyage up the river that bears his name. They founded the colony that later came to be known as New York. The Swedes staked out and tried to hold on to some territory along the Delaware.

When the Spaniards conquered Indian lands, they converted the Indians to the Catholic faith and forced them to labor in mines and on plantations. The French were interested in furs, not farming. They needed the Indians and did not wish to deprive them of their hunting land.

Since the English settlers came to the colonies to farm, they made clearings in the woods and fenced their property, thus cutting down the hunting lands left for the Indians. They looked upon the Indians as dirty, treacherous savages. Bad relations between the English and the Indians broke out almost everywhere the English settled.

15

SUSQUEHANNOCK
INDIANS

M A R Y L A N D

Potomac River

POWHATAN

INDIANS

Rappahannock River

V I R G I N I A

York River

Chickahominy River

BACON'S
PLANTATION

C H E S A P E A K E   B A Y

JAMESTOWN

James River

V I R G

JAMESTOWN
FOUNDED 1607
AND VICINITY

N

W ——— E

S

TROUBLE IN VIRGINIA

Take the first colony—the one at Jamestown in Virginia. The English settled in a low and swampy area (then a peninsula, now an island). It was covered with big trees and surrounded by unfriendly Indians who feared that the English would soon encroach on their land. These Indians belonged to various Algonquin tribes that had formed a confederacy and were ruled by a chief named Powhatan. The Indians looked upon the English as invaders, and the English were constantly on guard against Indian raids. They dared not go into the forests to hunt nor fish in the river and bay. In the early years, there was hunger and suffering, and the colony was on the verge of failure.

These times of trouble brought to the fore a real leader. His name was Captain John Smith. According to his own stories, he had fought against the Turks and enjoyed many hairbreadth escapes from danger, He also tells us that Powhatan's daughter, Pocahontas, loved him and saved his life when the Indian chief captured him and had his head placed on a big stone, ready to be bashed in.

Under Smith, the settlers built a blockhouse, erected cabins, and planted corn. The Indians found that the white settlers were there to stay. In 1614, Pocahontas married the Englishman John Rolfe. This resulted in what is known as the "married peace," and good relations between Indian and white lasted for the remainder of Powhatan's rule.

When Powhatan died, Opechancanough became the leader of most of the Indian nations of Virginia. He realized that the English were taking more and more land and planned to push the Indians farther into the interior. He felt that the time had come to strike and secretly planned a raid on the English.

The fateful morning came on March 22, 1622, when the Indians attacked and slew some 250 colonists. The English counterattacked, but they were not able to put an end to Indian raids until the 1630s. They were then too strong for the Indians to attack them.

In 1644, old Opechancanough led his followers in a second raid on the English, but he himself was captured and sent to Jamestown. There Opechancanough was slain by one of the settlers set to guard him. At long last the English conquered the great Powhatan Confederacy. The Indians were allotted lands in which to dwell and hunt and put themselves under the protection of the government of Virginia.

BACON'S REBELLION

For a time an uncertain peace lasted on the frontier of Virginia. Then, in 1675, a band of Doegs, an Algonquin

He was slain by one of the settlers set to guard him.

19

tribe from Maryland, killed some settlers on the Virginia frontier. A larger band of Susquehannocks soon invaded the colony. Indian raids took place the following winter. Hundreds of white settlers were killed. The people on the frontier were frightened, and they were angry, too, because greedy traders continued to sell powder, shot, and guns to the Indians although this was against the law.

Again Virginia found a leader to battle the Indians. This time he was a young man who had recently come from England. His name was Nathaniel Bacon. When the government of Virginia failed to put down the Indian attacks, Bacon raised three hundred volunteers. The governor of the colony at this time was Sir William Berkeley, a very old man who had ruled the colony for a very long time. He wanted peace with the Indians and did not approve Bacon's campaign. When Bacon attacked the Indians and slew 150 of them, Berkeley declared him a "rebel." Bacon then marched on Jamestown, the capital of the colony, and forced the governor to make him head of the militia. But the minute Bacon headed for the frontier, Berkeley again declared him an outlaw. So what had started out as a war to put down the Indians has become known to us as "Bacon's Rebellion," the first big uprising against any government of the English colonies.

Bacon's Rebellion took place in the year 1676, just one hundred years before the American Revolution. Bacon managed to drive Berkeley out of Jamestown. He then burned the town. A month later, Bacon fell ill and died. With his death, the rebellion was quickly put down by Berkeley's armed followers and most of the leaders of it put to death.

THE PILGRIMS, THE PURITANS, AND THE INDIANS

When the colonists settled in New England, the eastern branch of the Algonquins was torn apart by bitter rivalry. Shortly before the Pilgrims landed at Plymouth in 1620, a fierce Algonquin tribe known as the Pequots ("destroyers of men") came from the Hudson River region and spread fear and destruction among other Algonquin tribes. The Pequot stronghold was the Connecticut Valley. The Indians who had been in New England first were furious. The chief enemies of the Pequots were the Narragansetts, who held the land between Narragansett Bay and the western boundary of Rhode Island.

When the Pilgrims came to Plymouth, the Wampanoag Indians, an Algonquin tribe nearby, had been weakend by disease and did not try to fight them. Instead, they helped the Pilgrims with their planting and fishing.

The tribe known as the Massachusetts was also too weak to put up any resistance when the Puritans first settled the

21

colony of Massachusetts Bay in 1630. They looked upon the white settlers as allies against the Pequots. So did the Nipmucks, a tribe who lived in the interior of the colony.

The Narragansetts were friendly to the white settlers of Rhode Island because of the generous way they were treated by Roger Williams, the great statesman of that colony. Sassacus, the chief, or sachem (pronounced say'-chem), of the Pequots, had good reason to fear that the English would break his hold over the remaining Indian tribes.

In 1637, some tribes friendly to the Pequots staged a series of raids against Connecticut settlers living at Wethersfield. Connecticut called upon the other New England colonies for help. Massachusetts and Plymouth came to her aid. Roger Williams set out alone on a dangerous trip to see the chiefs of the Narragansetts and the Mohegans. Some Pequots were there ahead of him, but he persuaded his Narragansett and Mohegan friends to join the English side. The Pequots were left to fight the war without any important friends.

The New England forces were led by Captain John Mason. The troops approached the Pequot fort on the Mystic River at dawn. Not a sound was heard until Mason was a half dozen yards from the palisaded wall. Then a dog's bark shattered the stillness, and a Pequot's voice rang out: "Owanux! Owanux! Englishmen! Englishmen!" The

They hurled firebrands over the palisades.

English hurled firebrands over the palisades. Soon the village of seventy wigwams was ablaze.

The attackers formed two circles around the fort, ready to shoot down or scalp any Pequots who attempted to escape. The first ring was made up of Englishmen, the outer ring of Indian allies. In all, perhaps five hundred defenders perished, either caught in the blaze or riddled with musket fire or tomahawked by the Mohegans. "God is over us," Captain Mason shouted. "He laughs His enemies to scorn, making them as a fiery oven!"

The English lost two killed and twenty wounded. The Pequots who escaped headed for Manhattan, then a Dutch town. But Sassacus himself did not live long. He escaped to the Mohawks, but they took his scalp and sent it as a gift to Boston.

He escaped to the Mohawks.

THE NEW ENGLAND CONFEDERATION

New England was made up of a number of small English colonies. Would they be strong enough to stand up against another Indian attack? Moreover, the Dutch in New Netherland claimed land in the Connecticut Valley that was being settled by the English, and the French were threatening to push south from Canada. Suppose, the English asked themselves, the Dutch from the South and the French from the North were to attack at the same time as the Indians?

The fear of this possibility caused the four Puritan colonies of Connecticut, New Haven, Plymouth, and Massachusetts Bay to form a league in 1643. The real name of the league was "The United Colonies of New England," but it is always known as the New England Confederation. It was the first union of the colonies, and it lasted some forty years. The Confederation barred Rhode Island from membership because the Puritan colonies did not like the religious and political views of Roger Williams and the settlers of that colony. The league was formed to enable New England to fight united against any combination of enemies. It also proved to be a useful way to settle arguments over land boundaries between member colonies. Before it ended its career, the Confederation had to face a last great threat from the Indians.

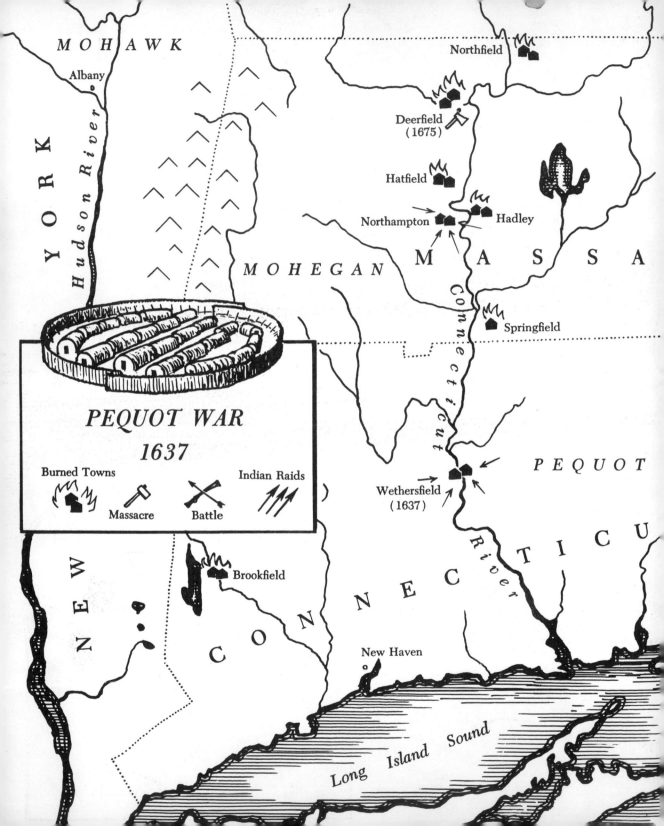

MOHAWK

Albany

Hudson River

NEW YORK

MOHEGAN

Northfield

Deerfield
(1675)

Hatfield

Northampton

Hadley

MASSA

Springfield

Connecticut River

PEQUOT WAR
1637

Burned Towns

Massacre

Battle

Indian Raids

Brookfield

Wethersfield
(1637)

PEQUOT

CONNECTICU T

New Haven

Long Island Sound

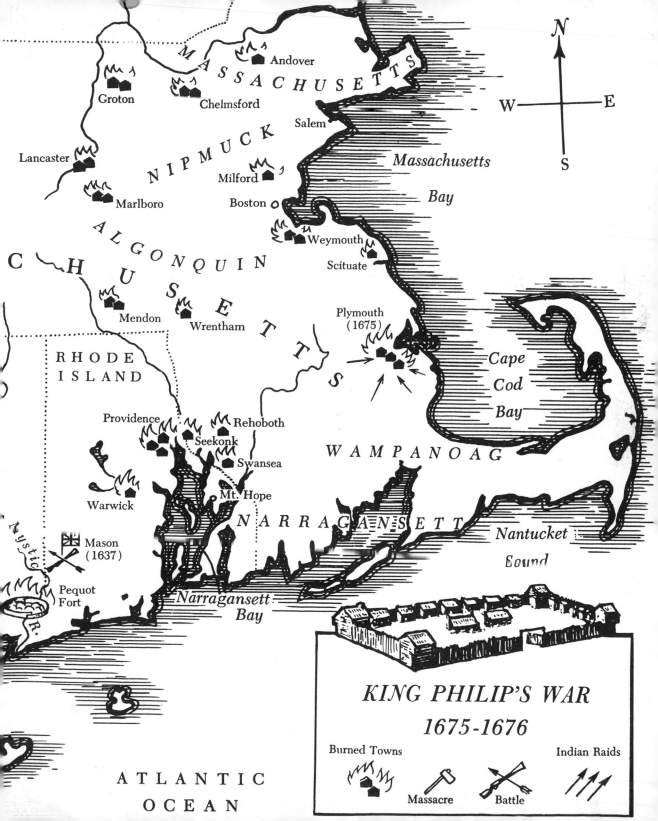

N
W — E
S

MASSACHUSETTS

Andover

Groton

Chelmsford

Salem

NIPMUCK

Massachusetts

Bay

Lancaster

Milford

Marlboro

Boston

ALGONQUIN

Weymouth

Scituate

CHUSETTS

Mendon

Wrentham

Plymouth
(1675)

Cape
Cod
Bay

RHODE
ISLAND

Providence

Rehoboth

Seekonk

WAMPANOAG

Swansea

Warwick

Mt. Hope

NARRAGANSETT

Nantucket
Sound

Mystic

Mason
(1637)

Pequot
Fort

Narragansett
Bay

KING PHILIP'S WAR
1675-1676

Burned Towns   Massacre   Battle   Indian Raids

ATLANTIC
OCEAN

KING PHILIP'S WAR

For a whole generation, the Indians lived at peace with the New England colonists. A goodly number were converted to Christianity by a Puritan minister, the Reverend John Eliot, who translated the Bible into the Indian tongues. These Christian Indians came to be called "praying Indians."

Trouble between the whites and the Indians broke out finally in the 1670s. To the south and southwest of the Plymouth settlement lived a tribe known as the Wampanoags. Their main fortified village was at the foot of Mount Hope, a hill behind the present town of Bristol, Rhode Island. Their sachem had been Massasoit, a long-time friend of the English. When he died, his younger son, known as King Philip, became sachem, and trouble soon followed.

The English in New England now numbered forty thousand; the Indians half that number. More and more land was being taken up by the English settlers. Philip told one Englishman: "But little remains of my ancestor's domain. I am resolved not to see the day when I have no country." He made up his mind that the English must not be allowed to spread any farther.

To rid the land of the English was too much for a single tribe. Philip set about holding parleys with the other

Algonquin tribes—all in secret. But his young braves could not be held back.

Raids against Plymouth colony started in the summer of 1675. The colonists, in turn, attacked Philip's stronghold, the Mount Hope peninsula, but Philip's Indians had already withdrawn. The war was too much for any colony alone. The New England Confederation now marshalled a force of one thousand soldiers to put down the Wampanoags. But the situation grew desperate as other tribes became restless. The Nipmucks joined Philip. The powerful Narragansetts seemed about to take to the warpath.

The English decided to attack the Indians before the Indians attacked them. In December 1675, they marched against the main Narragansett fort located in a great swamp along the eastern shore of Narragansett Bay. Setting fire to the wigwams in which the Indians were hiding, the English killed perhaps a thousand defenders, but they suffered heavily themselves. The Narragansetts now joined the Wampanoags and Nipmucks as open enemies of the English.

War now spread to the upper Connecticut Valley. Town after town was burned by the Indians, the white men slain, the women and children taken into captivity. Food became scarce. Men were called up to fight the Indians when they were in the midst of harvesting their crops. The Indians burned the local mills, which ground the grain into meal or flour. In desperation, the English placed military guards around some mills. More important, they decided to fight the Indians the Indian way— that is, to avoid pitched battles, use the woods for hiding and defense, and employ friendly Indians as scouts with every English force that moved through the woods.

The sad fact is that many of the friendly or "praying Indians" were cruelly treated by the white settlers during the war, just as many Americans of Japanese origin were unfairly treated when Japan attacked the United States in the Second World War. But the Indians remained faithful to their Christian religion.

Now the tide began to turn against the Indians. Canonchet, the Narragansett sachem, was captured when he attacked Plymouth and was put to death. The Narragansett support for King Philip crumbled. More and more of Philip's former allies sought to save their lives by making peace with the colonial governments.

Philip himself would not give up. The raids continued. In August of 1676, an informer told the veteran English fighter of Indians, Captain Benjamin Church, that Philip was hiding in a swamp on the southwestern side of Mount Hope. Church swiftly marched there, and threw his men in a circle around the Indian camp. At dawn they attacked. The Indians fell into a panic and fled. Philip himself tried to escape, but a ball from an Indian musket hit him, and he fell on his face in the mud and water with his gun under him. The shot had been fired by an Indian in the service of Captain Church.

Philip was killed not far from the rock where he had been crowned king of the Wampanoags. His head was cut off and sent to Plymouth. There it was put on a pole in front of the meeting-house. The Indian ringleaders who survived were also put to death, but Philip's wife and his nine-year-old son were captured and sold into slavery in the West Indies.

After almost three years of fighting the Indians were at last put down. Destruction was enormous. Many English towns were now only blackened ruins—Northfield, Deerfield, Lancaster, Groton, Warwick, among others, had been almost totally destroyed. Others, like Springfield and Providence, were badly scorched. In all, forty out of the ninety

He fell on his face in the mud and water.

towns in Massachusetts and Plymouth had been burned by the Indians and twelve destroyed entirely. Nearly one thousand white settlers lost their lives.

The war also took its toll on the Indians. Lives were lost and villages were destroyed. But, most important, the Indians had lost their battle for the land of their ancestors. Except for the Indians on the Maine frontier who joined with the French in border raids on New England, the Indians had disappeared from New England forever.

For years after King Philip's War people talked about the strange adventures of women and children who had been taken prisoner by the Indians and, in some cases, finally found their way home. Perhaps the most famous story was that of Mary Rowlandson. Her husband, the minister of the town of Lancaster, happened to be in Boston to beg the officials to provide his town with more protection. When he returned, he was shocked to find the town destroyed by the Indians and his family gone. The Indians had wounded both Mary Rowlandson and her infant, then carried them off as captives. After nine days, the baby died. During the twelve weeks Mrs. Rowlandson was with the Indians, they moved to twenty different encampments to keep from being captured by the English. Half-starved, the white woman lived on acorns and chestnuts and scraps of horsemeat. But she was not treated too badly. Finally, she was allowed to go home and rejoin her friends

The most famous story was that of Mary Rowlandson.

and relatives. Hers was a wonderful tale, and when it was printed shortly after the war, it quickly became a best seller.

THE IROQUOIS AND THE FRENCH

In the great wars between the French and the English for the control of North America, no tribe played a more important role than did the Iroquois of central New York. When the French came into the St. Lawrence Valley the Iroquois felt threatened. For a time, the Iroquois had forced the Algonquins and Hurons to accept their supremacy. Now these subject tribes preferred to sell their furs directly to the French rather than to let the Iroquois control their trade with the white man. In short, the Iroquois and the French hit it off badly from the start.

In 1609, the great French explorer Champlain invaded the Iroquois country on the lake that bears his name. Fighting between French and Iroquois broke out. In 1615, Champlain's men attacked an Onondaga village. This was fortified. There was a moat, or ditch filled with water, which ran around the village and a double wall or stockade. But the white men built a platform and moved it close to the walls. Then, from the platform, they could shoot over the stockade and bring terror and death to the defenders. The village was soon taken. So began a long enmity

KEY

- **French Forts** ▬
- **English Forts** ⌂
- ○ Cities   ✕ Battles

N

W   E

S

Hudson Bay

St. Lawrence River

Cape Breton Island

Louisbourg

E N G L I S H

Acadia (DISPUTED)

Port Royal

CHIPPEWA

CHIPPEWA

ALGONQUIN

Quebec

Lake Superior

HURON

Montreal

Lake Champlain

OTTAWA

Lake Huron

Lake Michigan

Lake Ontario

Ft. Ticonderoga

Lake George

Boston

F R E N C H   T E R R I T O R Y

Lake Erie

IROQUOIS

New York

Philadelphia

A T L A N T I C   O C E A N

Williamsburg

Ohio River

SHAWNEE

CHEROKEE

E N G L I S H   T E R R I T O R Y

CREEK

Mississippi

CHICKASAW

Charleston

CREEK

SPANISH TERRITORY

St. Augustine

CHOCTAW

New Orleans

FRENCH AND ENGLISH ADVANCES TO 1750

between the Iroquois and the French. This was to cost the French their empire in America.

The Iroquois turned to the Dutch for arms and got them. They then set out to capture the rich fur trade of the interior of the country. The Hurons and Algonquins controlled that trade, and the Iroquois planned to smash their rivals. They staged daring raids down the Champlain Valley, attacked the Hurons on the Richelieu River, and even raided the town of Montreal in the year 1644. Finally, the Hurons were badly beaten and forced to retreat as far west as Wisconsin, where they were joined by other tribes fleeing from the Iroquois attacks.

The Iroquois had won a tremendous victory, but the tribes they had defeated covered a great deal of ground, and the Iroquois could not hold on to their gains. The French now turned upon them and forced them to sue for peace. Some of the tribes that the Iroquois had forced out were now able to return to their old homes. But once the English were firmly established in New York, they encouraged the Iroquois to stage raids against their old enemies, both French and Indian. This was to keep the French from getting too firm a grip on the fur trade with the Great Lakes Indians. The Iroquois even raided the St. Lawrence Valley, and at the French town of Lachine they slaughtered two hundred persons in 1689 and took ninety prisoners.

WAR BETWEEN FRANCE AND ENGLAND

The man who stopped the Iroquois was a remarkable Frenchman named Count Frontenac, governor of New France. Frontenac had bold and big ideas about making France a great power in the New World. Under his leadership, the French pushed into the country of the Great Lakes and even down the Mississippi. These moves blocked further English expansion. In turn, the English established fur trading posts up north in Hudson Bay. They now could trade directly with the Indians of that region and keep their furs from going to the French along the St. Lawrence. The stage was set for a great clash between these two world powers, France and England.

Other reasons for war between the two powers could be found. Both the French and the English had for two centuries fished off the Grand Banks of Newfoundland, one of the greatest fishing areas in the whole world. After the catch, the fish would be dried out on land. The English used the lands around Newfoundland for this purpose. The French seized the nearby areas of Cape Breton and the Gaspé Peninsula. But outside of North America, too, France and England were rivals throughout the entire world. In Europe, France had the largest land forces, and other nations, chief among them England, made up their minds that France should not control Europe.

Four wars in all took place between France and England between 1689 and 1763. We speak of them as the Second Hundred Years' War. Sometimes they started in America. Sometimes the wars began because of some quarrel in Europe. France and England were not at war all the time, and the wars did not last quite a hundred years, but they were the real start of those world wars which have changed the face of our globe and have brought to the fore new powers like the United States and the Soviet Union.

In these four wars, France and England were very evenly matched. Of course, each side was stronger in some respects and weaker in others. The French in America had the advantage of being under one central control, unlike the English who were under thirteen or so colonial governments. The French in America had unity. The English colonists were divided. The French boasted the strongest army in Europe. In North America, they had well-placed forts protecting their holdings. These soon reached from the St. Lawrence in the northeast across the Great Lakes and down the great Mississippi River. The French counted on their woodsmen and fur traders who knew the forests and trails where the fighting would take place.

But in other respects, the English were stronger than the French. They had many more settlers in North America than the French. When war broke out in 1689, the English had one hundred thousand settlers in New England alone, while the French had only twelve thousand settlers in New France. The English also had a much bigger navy. England had more money to run a war and more and cheaper goods to trade with the Indians for their support.

At the start of the wars, the French counted on alliances with a great many Indian tribes. They had an unbroken chain of friends all the way from Maine to Wisconsin. Against them, the English could merely call upon their old friends, the Iroquois.

EARLY WARS BETWEEN THE COLONIES

The first war, which began in 1689 and ended in 1697, is known in America as King William's War, as William III was King of England when the war broke out. Under their great governor, Frontenac, the French and the Abenakis attacked the northern frontier and hit such widely scattered points as Sohenectady in New York, Falmouth (now Portland) and Wells in Maine, and Haverhill in Massachusetts. On their part, the English seized Port Royal in Nova Scotia. This attack was carried out by New England soldiers under the command of Sir William Phips with the support of the English navy. But the war ended in a stalemate—that is, neither side could defeat the other, and so each side gave back the territory it had captured.

Deerfield, Massachusetts, was destroyed in 1704.

Nothing had been settled, and, in 1702, the war broke out again in Europe when the English feared that the thrones of France and Spain would be united. The war soon spread to America, where it is called Queen Anne's War as she was on the English throne at that time. Again the Abenakis, stirred up by the French, hit the New England frontier. Deerfield, Massachusetts, was destroyed in 1704. Again the English captured Port Royal.

In the South, the English joined with Indian allies to seize and burn the Spanish town of St. Augustine in Florida, as Spain was fighting on France's side. Another English and Indian force tried to fight through to the Louisiana territory but was unable to knock out the Choctaw defenses that protected the French towns on the Gulf of Mexico. But England scored real gains in this war. By the Treaty of Utrecht (1713), she was given Newfoundland, Acadia, and Hudson Bay.

For more than twenty-five years, an uneasy peace prevailed between the French and English in America. Meanwhile, the French worked feverishly to settle the West. They founded New Orleans in 1718 and made numerous settlements in what are now the states of Indiana and Illinois. To add to English worries, the Indians of the southeast went on the warpath against English settlers and traders who pushed into their territory. To protect the southern frontier against the Spaniards and the Indians, the English set up the colony of Georgia, the most southerly and the last of the thirteen colonies to be founded.

Once more war started. This time it began between England and Spain in America, but France came into it on Spain's side very soon. The early part of the conflict is known as the War of Jenkins' Ear because a British ship captain named Jenkins claimed he had his ear cut off by Spanish coast guards.

Counting on the support of the friendly Creeks, Cherokees, and Chickasaws, James Edward Oglethorpe, the founder of Georgia, invaded Florida and destroyed a number of Spanish forts. Then war spread to Europe, with France coming in against England. In America, this war was known as King George's War because George II was King of England during that period.

The greatest event of King George's War was the capture of Louisbourg on Cape Breton Island. If you will look at the map, you will see that this strong French fortress stood at the gateway to the St. Lawrence. It fell to a joint expedition of New England soldiers headed by William Pepperrell and a fleet under Sir Peter Warren. Barefoot, tattered, and sick with fever, the New England men swarmed ashore, seized the main battery, and turned the cannon on the defenders. How disappointed the colonial soldiers were to find that their hard-won gains had to be turned back to the French by the treaty that ended this war. None of the outstanding differences between the French and the English had been settled.

PREPARATIONS FOR A SHOWDOWN

Both sides knew that peace could not last. There was bound to be a clash in the West. Both sides tried to get themselves ready for the shooting certain to come. The French built or strengthened a whole series of forts—one on Lake Ontario, another on Lake Erie, and a third on the upper St. Lawrence. But most important of all, they made strong efforts to win the Indians over to their side or to

The New England men swarmed ashore.

make sure that they would not join the English. From their posts in the southeast, the French visited Indian camps, smoked the peace pipe with the Chickasaws, and tried to win over the Creeks and the Cherokees.

England had cause for alarm. In the North, she had counted heavily on her old allies, the Iroquois. Originally the Five Nations, the Iroquois were now the Six Nations, since the Tuscaroras, a southern Indian tribe, had joined them. The Tuscaroras had come from North Carolina to New York after a bitter war with the settlers that had ended in 1712. But when the Iroquois looked to the North, the West, and the South, they saw everywhere a strong France. Once the French had built Fort Niagara on Lake Erie, the Iroquois felt it would be safer to be neutral—that is, not to take sides.

The English were now aroused by the French push in the West and South. They built Fort Oswego on Lake Ontario to oppose the French on Lake Erie and to reassure the Iroquois. They turned for help to an old friend of the Iroquois, William Johnson, an Indian trader and honorary sachem of the Mohawks, who, better than anyone, knew how to get along with the Six Nations.

William Johnson had spent his boyhood in Ireland and was considered a wild youth. His family sent him to his uncle's estate in the Mohawk country because they felt he was not fit for white society. But very soon, William showed himself to be a shrewd trader and land operator and became a great man in the Mohawk Valley. When he visited the Indians, he dressed and painted himself like an Indian brave. He made many friends among them and even took an Indian wife.

THE GREAT ALBANY CONGRESS

The English now saw two things. If they were to win the coming war against the French, they would have to get help from the Iroquois. They would have to get help, too, from the colonists. Together, England and the colonies would have to act with greater unity than they had in previous wars.

Time after time, England had called in vain on the colonies for money and fighting men, but the colonies were not likely to give much help unless they were directly threatened. Then some fought while others looked on. Some better way of raising a fighting force and collecting money to help run the war had to be worked out.

With these problems in mind, the English government issued a call for a Congress to be held in Albany. That Congress met in June of 1754. Some of the most famous colonists of that day attended. James De Lancey, lieutenant governor of New York, presided. From Massachusetts

45

"*You have thus thrown us behind your backs
and disregarded us.*"

46

came Thomas Hutchinson, already a prominent person, soon to become chief justice of his colony and then Tory governor, who took the side of the King against the Patriots. New York sent to Albany William Johnson, the best friend of the Iroquois. From Pennsylvania came the most famous of all the colonists of his day, Benjamin Franklin: printer, world-renowned scientist, and statesman.

The first business of the Congress was to make a treaty with the Iroquois. One hundred and fifty Indian chiefs attended. They bluntly told the English that they were not getting the protection from the English they had counted upon. "Look at the French," declared Chief Hendricks of the Mohawks. "They are men. They are fortifying everywhere. But—we are ashamed to say it—you are like women." Then he took a stick and threw it behind his back. "You have thus thrown us behind your back and disregarded us," he complained.

The English tried to calm the anger of the Indians. They promised to help them guard the frontier against the French. De Lancey gave a chain belt to the Indians to show that the colonies were acting together with all the Six Nations. The Iroquois chiefs left the conference much happier than when they came in. They had good reason to be. They departed with thirty wagonloads of presents, including guns.

Just as important to the English colonies, if not more so,

was the question of how to act in unity against the French and still keep their separate governments. Franklin, whose brain was never at rest, thought it was indeed strange that the Six Nations of Indians could form a union that had lasted for ages but a dozen or so English colonies could not act together for even a short time. He proposed that a union of the colonies be formed. At its head was to be a president-general appointed by the King in England and a Grand Council elected by the assemblies of each colony. Together, the president-general and the council would have the power to declare war and make peace and to make treaties with the Indians. There was to be a central treasury. This proposed central government would have the right to deal with the West, control land sales, raise armies, build forts, and levy taxes.

To win the people over to his plan, Franklin published in the *Pennsylvania Gazette* a cartoon showing a snake separated into parts, representing the colonies. Beneath it was the motto: "JOIN OR DIE." It was a pity that this plan for colonial unity was allowed to die, but Franklin was ahead of his time. The English government felt that the plan gave too much power to the colonies, and the colonial assemblies felt it gave too much power to the King. The idea was dropped. But it was to be brought up again at the time of the American Revolution. A number of its ideas are found in the Constitution.

GEORGE WASHINGTON'S MISSION

A race between France and England now started for control of the Ohio Valley. The French wanted to link their holdings in Canada with their settlements in the Illinois country and in Louisiana. Then the French settlers could join hands behind the backs of the English and keep the English from moving into the West. But the English colonists already had big plans for the West. In 1749, a group of Virginians had received a grant from the King of thousands of acres of land in the Ohio Valley. They began to urge settlers to move into that area.

To block the English, the French planned to build a chain of forts from Lake Erie to the Ohio. One of them, Fort Venango, was located on the site of a trading post that had been seized from the English. The Virginians were now alarmed. In 1753, their governor, Robert Dinwiddie, sent a young man named George Washington to Fort Venango to talk the French into leaving. Washington was just twenty-one years old, but he had been a surveyor of western lands, had lived on the frontier, understood the Indians, and knew how to lead men. He was also personally interested in western lands. The French were polite but firm. Their answer was: No. We are here to stay.

Early in 1754, Governor Dinwiddie sent Washington back to occupy a fort at the Forks of the Ohio, where the

Allegheny and the Monongahela Rivers join. Washington learned that the French were building a big fort at the Forks to be called Fort Duquesne after the French governor of Canada.

With a little band of 150 men, Washington met and defeated a scouting party of the French. Then he quickly built a crude stockade known as Fort Necessity. But the French proved too strong for him. A large force from Fort Duquesne attacked him, forced him to yield the post, but did not detain him as a prisoner.

And so, young Washington, who would one day lead the Continental army through eight long years of the American Revolutionary War, really fired the first shot in the last war between the colonies of France and England.

BRADDOCK'S DEFEAT

To capture Fort Duquesne and drive the French out of the Ohio Valley, the British sent to America General Edward Braddock with two crack regiments of soldiers. Braddock led the troops personally. Ahead of his forces went three hundred axmen to hack a road through the forest. George Washington, now a colonel, led 450 militiamen from Virginia who accompanied the British regulars.

Braddock fought bravely, but his was the old-style European warfare, not suited to the woods. With flags flying proudly and bagpipes shrilly playing, his forces were ambushed by the French and Indians about eight miles from Fort Duquesne. The bright-colored English uniforms made Braddock's men easy targets for the enemy marksmen, who fired from behind trees and under cover of thicket. Braddock had four horses shot from under him and then received a fatal wound. His forces fled in panic.

Now the Indians came out more openly in support of their French allies. For four hundred miles, the frontier of Virginia, Maryland, and Pennsylvania was ablaze. George Washington was given fifteen hundred men to defend this long line, and Washington acted with both wisdom and courage. But the task was too great. Outlying settlements frequently suffered from Indian massacres, and the English were pushed back to the Allegheny Mountains.

His was the old-style European warfare.

OTTAWA

Lake Huron

MICHIGAN

PONTIAC'S REVOLT
(1763)

HURON

HURON

Detroit

N
W   E
S

Ft. Toronto

Lake Ontario

Ft. Niagara

PONTIAC

Ft. Oswe

Lake Erie

WYANDOTTE

ERIE

CAYUGA

OHIO

Ft. Venango

I R O Q U O I S

ONON

COL. BOUQUET
(1764)

SHAWNEE

NEW

Chillicothe

[Ft. Pitt]
Ft. Duquesne

PENNSYLVANIA

LORD DUNMORE

BRADDOCK'S DEFEAT
(1755)

LEWIS

(1774)

Ohio River

COL. BOUQUET

Ft. Necessity

Pt. Pleasant

GEORGE
WASHINGTON

SUSQUEHANNA

MONETON

DELAWAR

MARYLAND

Philadelphia

CHEROKEE

Baltimore

NEW
JERSE

DELAWARE

VIRGINIA

MONACAN

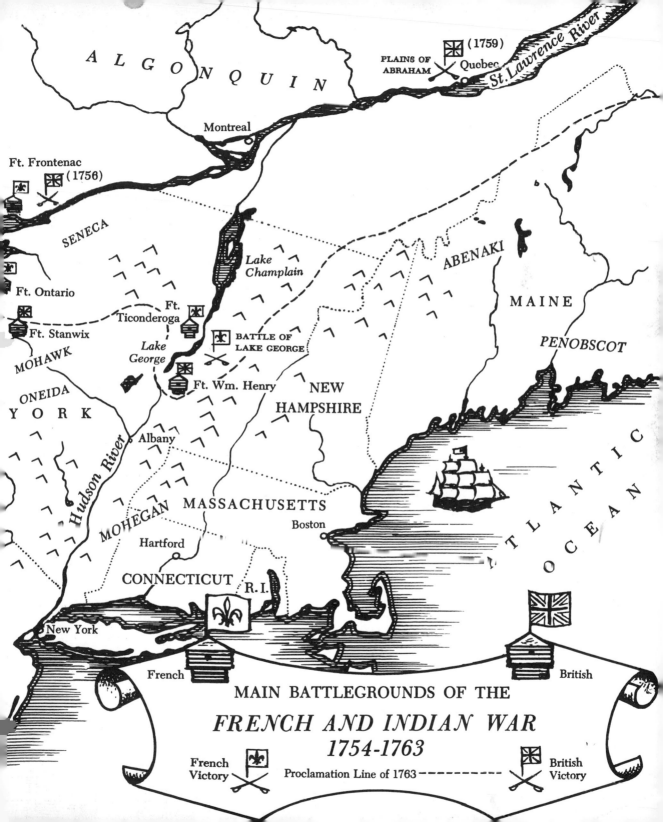

ALGONQUIN

St. Lawrence River

⚔ (1759)
PLAINS OF
ABRAHAM   Quebec

Montreal

Ft. Frontenac
⚜ ⚔ (1756)

SENECA

Ft. Ontario

Lake
Champlain

ABENAKI

MAINE

PENOBSCOT

Ft.
Ticonderoga

Ft. Stanwix

Lake
George

⚔ BATTLE OF
LAKE GEORGE

MOHAWK

Ft. Wm. Henry

ONEIDA

NEW
HAMPSHIRE

YORK

Hudson River

Albany

MOHEGAN   MASSACHUSETTS

Boston

Hartford

ATLANTIC

OCEAN

CONNECTICUT   R.I.

⚜

New York

French

British

MAIN BATTLEGROUNDS OF THE
FRENCH AND INDIAN WAR
1754-1763

French
Victory
⚜

Proclamation Line of 1763 — — — —

British
Victory
⚔

THE AMERICAN WAR BECOMES A WORLD WAR

The English and French colonists had been fighting some two years before England and France declared war on each other. This war, which is known as the French and Indian War in America, was called in Europe the Seven Years' War. The queen of Austria, Maria Theresa, hoped to regain the province of Silesia which Frederick the Great, King of the large German state of Prussia, had lately seized. So she joined forces with Russia and France against Prussia. England was already fighting France in America. But the King of England was also ruler of Hanover, a state in Germany. He was afraid that he would lose Hanover to this new combination of powers. So he joined forces with Prussia, his former enemy. What had begun as a local quarrel over the control of the Ohio Valley became a world war. It was fought in the West Indies, in Europe, and in Africa and India, where the French and English were rivals, as well as in North America. It was the first real world war of modern times.

MONTCALM IN COMMAND

A new general, the Marquis of Montcalm, was sent over early in 1756 to take command of the French forces in Canada. He had both ability and character. Looking over the situation, he saw that the English could still mount an attack on the French. They still held Fort Oswego on the south shore of Lake Ontario. As long as they held this, Fort Frontenac on the opposite side of the lake was in danger. If Fort Frontenac were to fall, the French line to the West would be cut in half.

Montcalm decided to attack Fort Oswego. The fort fell to the French, with its military stores and sixteen hundred prisoners. Now the French were in complete control of the Lake region. As a result, more and more Indians rallied to them.

There was another way of getting into Canada. That was through Lakes George and Champlain. Montcalm was taking no chances on an English attack from that direction. He fell upon Fort William Henry, the English fort at the lower end of Lake George. The English commander surrendered on the promise that the garrison would be taken safely to the English Fort Edward, sixteen miles away. But Montcalm could not control his Indian allies. A number of English captives were killed and scalped by the Indians and four hundred more kidnapped and held for ransom.

There was still a third way to get into Canada. That was through the St. Lawrence. Fort Louisbourg was the gateway which blocked this approach. The English attacked this fort but failed to capture it.

THE TIDE OF BATTLE TURNS

This was one of the darkest times in English history. The English now turned to William Pitt. He was known as the "Great Commoner" because he was a leading member of Parliament's lower house, the House of Commons. Pitt had ability and he knew it. "I know I can save this country and that no one else can," he boasted. He was right. In the fall of 1756, the King called him to the cabinet and, the next year, he was given entire control of the war.

Pitt laid his plans carefully. He reasoned that if Frederick the Great of Prussia could be helped, France would be tied down to fighting in Europe. Then England could turn to the main business at hand—expelling the French from North America. Pitt helped Prussia with money and troops. He shook up the English army and the navy. He picked young men to take the places of older men. Two of these young men were Jeffrey Amherst and James Wolfe.

Together, Amherst and Wolfe captured the fortress of Louisbourg in 1758. English and colonial soldiers fought together to take Forts Oswego and Frontenac from the French. The French now had lost their control over Lake Ontario and, with it, their links to their western posts. These victories really broke the French empire in half.

The war had started at the Forks of the Ohio. There, at Fort Duquesne, the French had kept control. Now under the British general John Forbes, a road was hacked through the forest to the French fort. Seeing that they could not defend it, the French blew up the fort. On this site, the British built Fort Pitt. Here, years later, was to arise the mighty city of Pittsburgh, named in honor of the brilliant English leader who turned the tide of battle when all seemed lost.

THE FALL OF QUEBEC

One of the great battles in the history of the world took place in Canada. It was the battle of Quebec. Whoever controlled Quebec had the key to all of Canada. Quebec was situated on a high bluff overlooking the St. Lawrence River. It could be reached on the river side only by climbing steep cliffs or by going through narrow ravines guarded by French troops. The French commander, Montcalm, was absolutely certain that Quebec could not be taken by assault.

To do the impossible, Pitt turned to James Wolfe. When one of the King's ministers remarked that Wolfe was a madman and not to be trusted with command, old George II replied: "Mad is he? Then I hope he will bite some others of my generals."

In June 1759, General Wolfe, with ships carrying sixteen thousand men, dropped anchor in the river before the fortress of Quebec. For two months, he tried to lure Montcalm into coming out and fighting. But the Frenchman was crafty and would not leave his fortifications. If only he could hold out until winter, he knew that the English would have to raise the siege and withdraw their fleet.

Wolfe knew he could not wait. He must try a bold stroke. On the night of September 12, a landing party went ashore two miles above Quebec and overcame a small force guarding the ravine. Before morning, forty-five hundred British soldiers had clambered up the cliff to an area of level land called the Plains of Abraham (named after a river pilot, Abraham Martin, who once had owned land there). From there, the English were in a position to cut off Montcalm's supplies, which came into Quebec from up the river.

Montcalm decided to fight immediately rather than to await reinforcements. He felt that if he started the battle quickly, Wolfe would not have time to bring up all his troops. But he was mistaken. Wolfe had his entire fighting force with him already. The French were outgunned, outnumbered, and less experienced than the British regulars.

On the morning of June 13, the battle began. Before going into battle, Wolfe recited the poem of the famous English poet, Thomas Gray, called "An Elegy Written in a Country Churchyard." He then told his fellow officers:

British soldiers clambered up the cliff.

"Gentlemen, I had rather have written those lines than take Quebec."

One of the most moving lines in the poem was: "The paths of glory lead but to the grave." That day Wolfe and Montcalm both gained glory and both died on the field of battle. Seeing the enemy fleeing everywhere, the dying Wolfe said: "Now, God be praised. I will die in peace!" Those were the last words of this gallant Englishman. Four days later, Quebec fell. In the following year, Montreal surrendered to the three English armies that converged on it. The war in America was over.

THE TREATY OF PARIS OF 1763

Everywhere the British were victorious. They smashed the French fleet on the seas. In Africa, they ended the French traffic in slaves. In India, they brought an end to French influence. By the Treaty of Paris that ended the war, England acquired Canada and all of France's territory east of the Mississippi except New Orleans. Two great sugar-producing islands in the West Indies that England had seized—Martinique and Guadeloupe—were returned to France, as well as Haiti. Cuba and the Philippine Islands, which the British had taken, were given back to Spain. That nation had come into the war on France's side when the shooting was almost over. She turned over Florida to England. To reward Spain in some way for her help, France gave her New Orleans and the lands west of the Mississippi known as Louisiana. France still kept two tiny islands off the coast of Newfoundland that could be used for drying fish, for she also kept the privilege of fishing off the Grand Banks.

PONTIAC'S CONSPIRACY

The greatest historian of the French and Indian War, Francis Parkman, once wrote: "With the fall of Quebec began the history of the United States. The French could no longer block the movement west, and the Indians were to be less and less of a threat." But this did not happen right away.

The Indians were shocked by the defeat of France. They would not accept it. A Chippewa chief said: "Englishmen, although you have conquered the French, you have not conquered us." The Indians were alarmed by reports that the English were going to set up colonies for their settlers west of the mountains. Land promoters set about making big plans to slice up the Indian hunting lands. The French traders who remained in the West added fuel to the fire. They told the Indians that a French army was on its way to win back the Ohio Valley for the French and the Indians.

The chief of the tribe of Ottawas around Detroit was a bold and eloquent brave named Pontiac. He believed that the settlers should be driven out of the forest and the Indians should return to the way they had lived before the colonists came. Pontiac's aim was to seize the scattered forts and wipe out the frontier settlements at harvest time so that the settlers would starve. He formed a confederacy of western tribes and started the biggest Indian uprising in American history. The Shawnees and the Delawares were his most loyal allies, but even one tribe of the Iroquois joined with him.

Pontiac struck suddenly in 1763. Soon the whole frontier was ablaze. Several thousand settlers were killed. Every English fort in the West except Forts Pitt, Niagara, and Detroit were captured by the Indians. Finally, the English rallied under Colonel Henry Bouquet. They marched from Fort Pitt into Ohio and smashed the uprising. Then William Johnson, the old friend of the Indians, stepped in and made a treaty with Pontiac. Peace returned to the frontier.

THE PROCLAMATION LINE OF 1763

The British were alarmed by the turn of affairs. They wanted to keep peace with the Indians. If the Indians were undisturbed in their hunting grounds, the rich fur trade would continue to flourish. The King issued a proclamation in 1763 that drew a line along the crest of the Appalachians. Settlement by English colonists west of the line was forbidden for the time being. People already there were expected to leave. At some future time, the English would open the land to settlement after first purchasing it from the Indians.

Needless to say, the colonists were angered by this action. Like George Washington, they wanted to obtain the new lands of the West and felt that the British government was depriving them of their rights. On the other hand, the Indians were happy about it.

Instead of fighting the Indians, the English and the colonists wisely set about making peace with them. By treaties they obtained new lands from the Indians. The Iroquois were induced to give to the English whatever rights they had to certain land in central New York and to a large area covering southwestern Pennsylvania, West Virginia beyond the Alleghenies, and the region between the Ohio and the Tennessee Rivers. Another treaty was made with the Cherokees by which Virginia's border was pushed farther west. The Creeks agreed with the settlers of Georgia on a dividing line between English and Creek territory.

Now the settlement of the West could begin in earnest.

By 1770, the young town of Pittsburgh could boast twenty log cabins, and a village already stood on the present site of Wheeling, West Virginia. Pioneers like John Sevier in Tennessee and Daniel Boone in Kentucky were to make history on the frontier.

LORD DUNMORE'S WAR

As the settlers began to build more and more cabins on Indian hunting grounds south and east of the Ohio, the Indians became more and more uneasy. At last, fighting broke out on the northwestern frontier of Virginia. It was started by the Shawnees, but other tribes joined the war.

Virginia bore the brunt of the fighting. Her governor, Lord Dunmore, sent out two military forces to attack the enemy. The governor himself headed one of them. The other was led by General Andrew Lewis. Both were to meet at the mouth of the Kanawha River. But Dunmore changed his plans and encamped at Pickaway Plains near the Indian town of Chillicothe.

General Lewis assembled an army of frontiersmen. Dressed in hunting shirts and wearing moccasins, they looked more like Indian braves than English soldiers. But they were brave, they were crack marksmen, and they knew how to fight the Indians.

General Lewis assembled an army of frontiersmen.

When Lewis came to the mouth of the Kanawha River, he got Dunmore's message to break camp and join him at Pickaway Plains. But he learned that close by his own position lay nearly a thousand Indians, armed and ready for battle. They were led by Cornstalk, chief of the Shawnees. A bloody battle took place at Point Pleasant, and the Shawnees were beaten. They surrendered all their prisoners and gave up all their claims to the land south and east of the Ohio River.

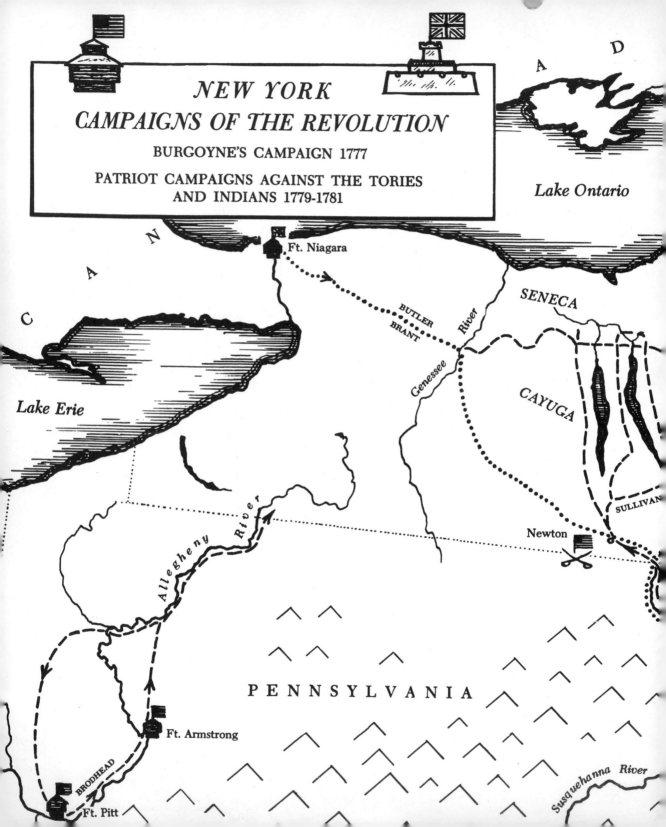

NEW YORK
CAMPAIGNS OF THE REVOLUTION

BURGOYNE'S CAMPAIGN 1777

PATRIOT CAMPAIGNS AGAINST THE TORIES
AND INDIANS 1779-1781

Lake Ontario

Lake Erie

Ft. Niagara

BUTLER
BRANT

SENECA

Genessee River

CAYUGA

SULLIVAN

Newton

C A N A D A

Allegheny River

PENNSYLVANIA

Susquehanna River

Ft. Armstrong

BRODHEAD

Ft. Pitt

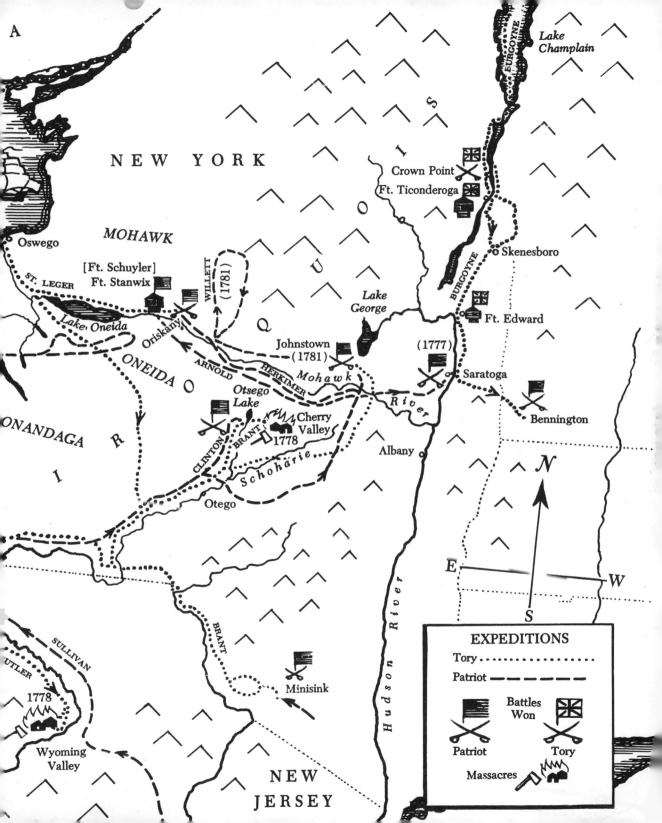

A

Lake Champlain

New York

Crown Point
Ft. Ticonderoga

Oswego

MOHAWK

[Ft. Schuyler]
Ft. Stanwix

WILLETT (1781)

Skenesboro

ST. LEGER

Lake Oneida

Oriskany

ONEIDA

Lake George

Ft. Edward

BURGOYNE

ARNOLD

HERKIMER

Johnstown
(1781)

Mohawk

River

(1777)

Saratoga

ONANDAGA

Otsego
Lake

Bennington

CLINTON

BRANT

1778

Cherry
Valley

Albany

Schoharie

N

Otego

E
W
S

SULLIVAN

BRANT

UTLER

1778

Minisink

Wyoming
Valley

Hudson River

EXPEDITIONS

Tory . . . .

Patriot ― ― ― ―

Battles
Won

Patriot

Tory

Massacres

NEW
JERSEY

INDIAN FIGHTING IN THE AMERICAN REVOLUTION

Just as the Indians had reasons to quarrel with the colonists, so the colonists had more and more reasons to quarrel with England. Finally, shooting broke out at Lexington and Concord in April 1775. The colonists realized that they would have to fight to defend themselves and that the only way they could win their rights was by becoming entirely free of English control. The American Revolution had begun. It lasted eight long years, and the end of it found the United States a free and independent nation.

How did the Revolution affect the Indians, and what part did they take in it? The Indians had come to look upon the colonial settlers as their enemies. The settlers wanted the Indians' hunting lands for their own, and the Indians were being forced more and more into the interior of the country. They had come to look upon the King of England as their protector against the colonists. It was the King who tried to check the westward rush of settlers after the French and Indian War and who tried to stop land grabbing and crooked trading with the Indians. Moreover, the English had the supplies, the articles for trade, and the fur-trading posts. That is why, in most cases but not all, the Indians took up the tomahawk for the English and wielded it against the Patriots.

BURGOYNE'S CAMPAIGN

In certain campaigns the English used the Indians much more than in others. One of the best known examples of a mixed force of British regulars, Tories, and Indians was General John Burgoyne's campaign to capture New York state and divide the colonies into two parts. In June of 1777, Burgoyne moved across the Canadian border to Lake Champlain. His force of seven thousand included four hundred Indians. He gathered the Indians together on the shores of Lake Champlain and called on them to fight. He forbade them to kill prisoners or women, children, and aged men. When he finished speaking, an old Iroquois chief rose up and replied:

"We have been tried and tempted by the Bostonians, but we have loved our father, and our hatchets have been sharpened upon our affections." Then all the Indians shouted the ancient war cry

Burgoyne's speech shocked the civilized world. In the English Parliament, Edmund Burke laughed at the appeal. He compared Burgoyne to a keeper of wild animals who opens the gates and then tells the beasts: "My gentle lions—my humane bears—my tender-hearted hyenas go forth!" Pitt protested: "We turn loose these savage hell-hounds!"

The warnings of Burke and Pitt proved correct. Once the Indians had joined the English, it was hard to make

She was shot and scalped.

them behave. In the course of the southward march of the British army through a trackless wilderness, some Indians captured a young woman named Jane McCrea. She was shot and scalped, and her murderer, an Indian named Wyandot Panther, was pardoned by Burgoyne. This atrocity did more to arouse the whole North country against Burgoyne than any other act of his campaign.

70

While Burgoyne's big army was lumbering southward through the forests, a mixed force of eighteen hundred men, mostly Tories and Indians, under Colonel Barry St. Leger, pushed eastward from Fort Oswego on Lake Ontario to join with Burgoyne in Albany. St. Leger was first held up by the Americans at Fort Stanwix on the Mohawk River. General Nicholas Herkimer marched to the fort's relief, but he was caught in an ambush at Oriskany by a force of Indians and Tories led by the Mohawk chief Joseph Brant. Herkimer suffered a wound from which he later died but held off the Indians until they were alarmed by firing from Fort Schuyler and scampered for safety.

The Patriot general Philip Schuyler now sent Benedict Arnold to the relief of the garrison. Arnold employed a clever ruse. An eccentric, half-mad settler named Hon Yost Schuyler was captured by Arnold's men while attempting to get them to join the British forces. He was sentenced to death but let off on condition that he use his special powers among the red men to make St. Leger's Indians desert. It seems that Hon Yost's strange actions and ravings had led the Indians to regard him as a prophet. He got into the Indian lines and told them that the Tories had been badly beaten. The Indians then ran away, and St. Leger had to retreat to Lake Oswego.

With St. Leger in retreat, and no real help coming from New York City, Burgoyne's situation now became hopeless.

His Indian and Tory forces faded away, and he was finally cornered and forced to surrender in October 1777, at the Battle of Saratoga. This battle is one of the turning points of world history. It showed the world that the Patriots could beat the best English fighting men and caused the French to come into the war on the side of the Americans.

FRONTIER WARFARE DURING THE REVOLUTION

Had the British organized Indian fighting and timed Indian attacks to take place on the whole frontier at the same time as the British struck at Boston, New York, and Charleston, the war might have ended differently. But happily for the Americans, the British lacked such a master plan.

Along the borders, terrible damage was inflicted by the Indians. Fierce raids were staged in the Susquehanna, Mohawk, and Schoharie Valleys, and Kentucky was attacked again and again. But probably the most horrible raid occurred in the Wyoming Valley, along the banks of the Susquehanna, near present-day Wilkes-Barre, Pennsylvania. In July 1778, a force of Tories and Indians struck. They were twelve hundred strong. Against them, Colonel Zeb Butler could muster only three hundred men and boys. Butler foolishly let his men leave the protection of Forty Fort to seek battle in the open. They were caught in ambush and destroyed. Then the Wyoming settlements were put to the torch, and many of the settlers killed.

Another raid soon followed against Cherry Valley, near Otsego Lake, New York. Many women and children were killed and all the houses burned. The leader of this raid was the Indian known as Joseph Brant.

GENERAL SULLIVAN STRIKES BACK

In the spring of 1779, General Washington picked General John Sullivan to attack the Indian country. One column, under Sullivan, moved up the Susquehanna to the New York border; another, under General James Clinton, struck across the Mohawk Valley, down Otsego Lake, and down the Susquehanna. A third, under Colonel Daniel Brodhead, advanced from Pittsburgh up the Allegheny into the Indian country.

In August, the combined forces met an army of Indians and Tories, smashed them, and drove them from the field. They then burned the standing grains, destroying the Indians' food supply. But raids along the New York borderlands continued. Finally, in the fall of 1781, Colonel Marinus Willett, a tough frontier fighter, met the Indians and Tories at Johnstown, defeated them, and swept them west to Oswego.

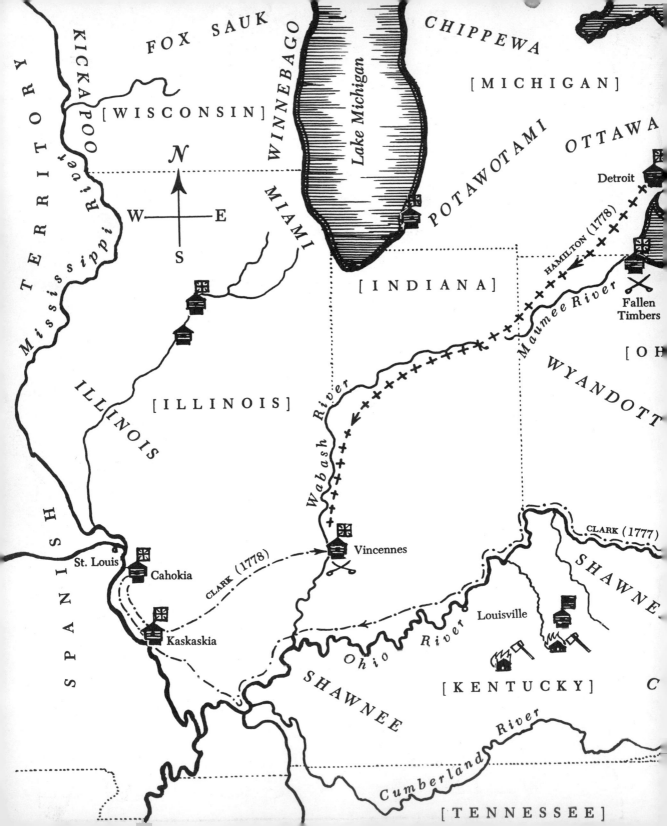

HURON

Ft. Toronto

Lake Ontario

Oswego

Ft. Schuyler

I R O Q U O I S

Ft. Niagara

F I V E   N A T I O N S

N E W   Y O R K

Cherry
Valley
Massacre
(1778)

Lake Huron

Lake Erie

Wyoming Valley
Massacre
(1778)

P E N N S Y L V A N I A

Susquehanna *River*

[O]

Ft. Pitt

PROCLAMATION LINE OF 1763

Ft. Redstone

S H A W N E E

V I R G I N I A

[ROKEE

*NORTHWEST CAMPAIGNS
OF THE AMERICAN REVOLUTION
1778-1783*

Indian
Raids

Battles

Forts

THE CONQUEST OF THE OLD NORTHWEST

At Detroit, the British commander Colonel Henry Hamilton kept stirring up the Indians against the Patriots. Reports had it that he was offering the Indians large bounties for American scalps. He was nicknamed "the Hair Buyer." Had it not been for one man, George Rogers Clark, Kentucky would have been overwhelmed by the Indians. Only twenty-three years old when the war broke out, Clark had been a surveyor and Indian fighter. He worked out a plan for saving Kentucky by conquering the Northwest. This meant capturing the British forts at Vincennes, Detroit, and Michilimackinac. Governor Patrick Henry of Virginia liked Clark's plan and made him a colonel in the Virginia forces.

With less than two hundred men, Clark floated down the Ohio to a point below Louisville, marched overland to Kaskaskia in southern Illinois, and captured it without a struggle. Then Cahokia, nearby, surrendered, and so did Vincennes in southwestern Indiana.

Colonel Hamilton then swept down from Detroit with an army of a thousand Indians and regulars. He recaptured Vincennes, but not for long. Clark now wrote an exciting chapter in the history of the West. In February 1779, he set out from Kaskaskia with 150 men. He marched across flooded and sometimes ice-covered plains to the outskirts

Clark floated down the Ohio.

of Vincennes. He then frightened off many of the enemy's Indian allies and forced Hamilton to surrender.

MAKING PEACE ON THE FRONTIER

While the winning of the peace was beneficial to the colonists, it created new problems for the Indians. The Treaty of 1783 between the United States and Great Britain gave America all land west to the Mississippi River and north to the Great Lakes, without regard to the Indian claims to the land. The Iroquois agreed to yield their claims to all land west of the Niagara River. The Chippewas, Delawares, Ottawas, and Wyandots gave up their claims to virtually the whole state of Ohio, except for a small reservation. But some of the other Ohio tribes, notable among them the Shawnees, stubbornly held out. Finally, the Shawnees signed a treaty giving up their claims as far west as the Wabash River. But then they changed their minds, and in the spring and summer of 1786, Indian raids took place on the western frontier.

In the Southwest, the Creeks agreed that Georgia's state line could be moved west to the Oconee River. Then they denounced the pact, and, under Chief Alexander McGillivray, a half-breed who hated whites, they began war against the Georgians. The Creeks were beaten in 1785 and forced to agree to the previous terms. But at best, an uneasy peace prevailed on the Southern frontier.

The main cause of continued trouble on the frontier was the refusal of England to give up the chain of forts she held along the Great Lakes. Chief among these were Oswego, Niagara, and Detroit. By the Treaty of 1783, England was supposed to move out of American territory "with all convenient speed," but the British refused to do so on the ground that America had not carried out its part under the treaty. The United States had not seen to it that British merchants were paid the moneys owing to them from before the American Revolution and had not stopped the states from seizing the properties of Tories. But the real reason the British did not give up the posts was because they wanted to hold on to the rich fur trade with the Indians. They kept the Indians supplied with arms and constantly egged them on to attack frontier settlements.

Peace on the frontier was brought about by force of arms and by agreement. In 1794, the American General Anthony Wayne defeated the Indians at Fallen Timbers on the Maumee, near what is now Toledo. The Indians were now broken in spirit and surrendered their rights to most of what is now Ohio.

Two treaties soon followed. John Jay, a famous New Yorker and Chief Justice of the United States Supreme Court, made a treaty with England in 1794 by which the

Much had been done to bring about peace on the frontier.

English agreed to get out of the posts. Then, two years later, Thomas Pinckney of South Carolina made a treaty with Spain that allowed the United States to have the free navigation of the Mississippi River and also obtained from the Spaniards a promise that they would keep Indians living on Spanish territory from attacking American settlements.

By the time George Washington had left the office of the Presidency, much had been done to bring about peace on the frontier, but not always by the fairest methods. During the next few generations, many Indians were forcibly removed and settled on reservations, areas of land supposedly reserved for and governed by Indians. These actions marked a shameful episode in U.S. history when the Indians felt continually forced to fight for the right to live in peace. Wars between Indians and white settlers continued until 1890.

It is the duty of the federal courts to see that the rights of Indians are protected. In some cases, the U.S. government has awarded Indians large sums of money for lands taken from them years ago in violation of treaties. But by no means have all the wrongs done to the Indians been righted. Since 1924, citizenship has been extended to all Indians. And that is as it should be. For they are truly the very first Americans.

INDEX

84

RICHARD B. MORRIS, Gouverneur Morris Professor of History Emeritus at Columbia University, is one of the United States' foremost authorities in the field of American history. He has also taught or lectured at many other universities, including Princeton, the University of Hawaii, and the John F. Kennedy Institute in West Berlin, and is a three-time recipient of a Guggenheim Fellowship. In addition, Dr. Morris is editor of the *Encyclopedia of American History* and the author of numerous books, including the Bancroft Award winner, *The Peacemakers*, and *Witnesses at the Creation: Hamilton, Madison, Jay, and the Constitution*. Presently, he is co-chair of *Project '87*, a nationwide organization devoted to commemorating the 200th anniversary of the U.S. Constitution.

AMERICAN HISTORY TOPIC BOOKS

The American Revolution
The Constitution
The Founding of the Republic
The Indian Wars
The War of 1812